# Contents

## Introduction

## Section 1: How to Decide What to Research

## Section 2: How to Carry Out Research

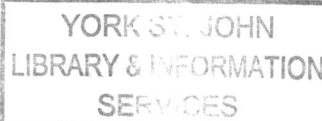

## Section 3: How to Evaluate and Present Research

## Section 4: Extra Resources

# Introduction

*First, some words of warning...*

1. This pack has been written with several syllabuses in mind. It offers resources which could be appropriate for the A level Media Studies and Film Studies research units of the major exam boards. Remember to check with your own syllabus and teacher to find out what material in the pack is relevant to your own syllabus requirements.

2. Plagiarism or 'deliberate deception', where you use the work of others as if it is your own is treated very seriously by exam boards and may result in your work being penalised. You need to know that there are several methods, including specialist software, which can identify work containing plagiarism. Make sure you give full and proper credit to material which is not your own. Some students plagiarise out of carelessness rather than through deliberate intent, but you need to be scrupulous with every stage of your work to ensure you cannot be accused of plagiarism.

   The simple solution is to record details of every source you come across and to give full and appropriate credit to the work of others, through quoting their work and attributing ideas to their writers. Using quotations and referring to the work of others will then bring you credit as it shows that you have read widely and considered a range of ideas.

3. Observe Health and Safety issues at all times, considering the welfare of yourself and others. Do not put yourself or others at risk. Discuss these issues with your teacher, but you need to consider a range of issues, from contacting strangers to the safe use of computers.

4. Familiarise yourself with the ethics of conducting research, particularly where children are concerned. Key aspects include the necessity of **full and informed consent** from your participants and an **avoidance of harm**. You will need to design a consent form detailing what your research will involve and the rights of your participants; this will need to be signed by your participants / their parents or guardians.

Before you begin, look at the following sites which give relevant information on Health and Safety and Ethical issues:

- www.bera.ac.uk — British Educational Research Association.
- www.bps.org.uk — British Psychology Society.
- www.buckscc.gov.uk/schools/infopoint/policies_and_guidance/photographs.asp — Buckinghamshire County Council (an example of advice on use of photos in schools).
- www.chronicpoverty.org/CPToolbox/ — Chronic Poverty Research Centre.
- www.safety.ngfl.gov.uk/schools/documentphp3?D=d74 — DfES Superhighway Safety.
- www.the-sra.org.uk (then follow link to Ethical Guidelines) — Social Research Association.

**What do I know about research, investigative essays or carrying out an independent study?**

You are already a researcher. At some point in your education so far, you will probably have done some or all of the following:

1. Found out what people think via questionnaires or interviews.

2. Discussed these ideas with others.

3. Researched books, magazines and the Internet for more information.

4. Written up and presented a project.

You have already built up skills in finding, reading, sorting, discussing, analysing and presenting information and ideas. All of these skills will be essential for research into the media.

Research, investigative essays or independent study means looking more deeply into a topic on your own under supervision.

**Why do I need to carry out research?**

You are probably reading this because your exam syllabus requires you to carry out research, an investigative essay or an independent study into some aspect of the media. As part of your course, you may have to complete research in the form of coursework or prepare it in advance to write it up in an exam situation. Depending on your syllabus, you may need to write in a different style to essay writing, perhaps using the first person ('I carried out research into…'). You will probably have to focus on key media concepts and you may need to consider theoretical models, that is, research already carried out by experts. Whatever you do, you will need to pay as much attention to your methodology as to your content. Your syllabus may specify the research methods to be used and they could be any of the following: textual analysis, primary research, content analysis, audience research, industry research, secondary research, quantitative or qualitative research. Always check your syllabus for what you are allowed to do.

**Apart from exams, what are the benefits of learning how to do research or an independent study?**

1. Research teaches independent learning skills.

2. Research creates a forum for discussion.

3. Research brings new ideas, which is very important for developing subjects like Media Studies and Film Studies.

4. Research is a feature of many Higher Education courses, so getting it right now will stand you in good stead.

5. Research gives you opportunities to develop your analytical skills.

6. Research is a key element of many jobs in the media, for example, researching potential audiences, piloting programmes and seeking audience feedback.

7. Research helps develop your ICT skills, both in terms of finding and presenting material.

8. Each piece of research is unique: what you write will never be exactly the same as somebody else's work.

**What can this pack offer me?**

The suggestions, activities and approaches in this pack have been written particularly with GCSE and A level students in mind, but you should also find something useful in here if you are working at a different level. Some activities have been differentiated, so you can be guided towards the one that is right for you at this stage.

Whatever your level, this pack offers ideas for 3 key aspects of research:

1. How to decide what to research.

2. How to carry out research.

3. How to organise, analyse, present, reflect on and evaluate your research.

The activities in this pack have been organised into an appropriate order, but you may prefer to choose your own route.

# Some current requirements of Exam Boards

| EXAM BOARD | TITLE OF RESEARCH UNIT | ASSESSMENT |
|---|---|---|
| **OCR – Media Studies** www.ocr.org.uk Check Assessment Objectives on the website and in the syllabus. | Critical Research Study. Worth 15% of A2 grade. | • A2 module. • 2 hour exam. • 2 questions, one on your research methodologies, the other on analysis of your research. • Permitted to take 4 sides of handwritten notes into the exam. • Some choice within a range of set topics. |
| **AQA – Media Studies** www.aqa.org.uk Check Assessment Objectives on the website and in the syllabus. | Independent Study. Worth 20% of A2 grade. | • A2 module. • Coursework. • 3,000 word essay. • Either a contemporary media text or texts or a topic or issue arising out of or suggested by a contemporary media text or texts. • 'Contemporary' = produced or released within the previous 2 years. • Text(s) should be appropriately contextualised. • Must refer to key concepts. |
| **WJEC – Media Studies** www.wjec.co.uk Check Assessment Objectives on the website and in the syllabus. | Investigating Media Texts. Worth 20% of A2 grade. | • A2 module. • Coursework. • 2,000–3,000 word investigative or analytical essay. • Focus on one or more of the following concepts: genre, narrative form, representation. • Work should be based on no more than 3 texts. |
| **WJEC – Film Studies** www.wjec.co.uk Check Assessment Objectives on the website and in the syllabus. | Auteur Research Project and Presentation (part of the Film – Making Meaning 2 module). Worth 20% of A2 grade. | • Part of an A2 module (the other half of the module is Creative Work). • Coursework. • Project and Presentation. • Research motivated by a problematic which is stated in the form of a proposal. • Catalogue of materials (generally 6–20 items) and 1,000 word evaluation. • Presentation script outline. • Reference to a group of at least 3 films. |

## TOP TIP

Keep the following 7 points in mind when carrying out research:

1. CONSENT – Ensure you have full and informed consent from your participants.

2. COURTEOUS – Make it a pleasant experience.

3. CONFIDENTIAL – Change names if your participants want you to.

4. CAREFUL – Be careful when meeting people in real life or via the Internet.

5. CHILDREN – Get proper permission from parents/guardians/teachers.

6. COPYRIGHT – Check what is copyrightable, including the Internet.

7. COST – What costs might be involved? Could this research make money for you?

## 1.1 ASKING THE RIGHT QUESTIONS

How much do you know already? As a media student and someone who has been a consumer of the media for all of your life, you already have a body of knowledge, which you can now build upon in your research.

This activity makes use of the set of 6 questions which many journalists ask when researching a story:

**WHAT?**                    **WHERE?**                    **WHY?**

**WHO?**                     **WHEN?**                     **HOW?**

Here are some examples of the information journalists might need:

- WHAT HAPPENED? Road traffic accident? Music festival? Jumble sale?

- WHO WAS INVOLVED? Casualties? Celebrities? Community group?

- WHERE DID IT TAKE PLACE? Motorway? Country park? Social hall?

- WHEN DID IT HAPPEN? Rush hour? Last night? Last week?

- WHY DID IT HAPPEN? Poor visibility? Long-standing tradition? Charity fundraiser?

- HOW DID IT HAPPEN? Police report? Interview with organisers? Who put in all the work?

As a researcher, you will need to ask many questions to obtain the information you need. As students, you will already know something about the media and this activity is designed to demonstrate how much you already know and also how much you need to know.

Here are some suggestions for how media students could approach the 6 questions:

- WHAT: What the debate is, e.g. violence on TV, postmodernism, children's television genres.

- WHO: Who this topic concerns, e.g. theorists, female audiences, major institutions.

- WHERE: Where the debate centres, e.g. UK or global, urban or rural, mainstream or sub-cultures.

- WHEN: Anything to do with time, e.g. contemporary or historical, key dates, duration of research studies.

- WHY: Why the situation came about, e.g. relaxation of censorship, interactive TV, increase in home cinema.

- HOW: What actually happened, how research was done and what results it came up with.

**1.1**

## SOLO ACTIVITY

Choose one of the following media topics and complete the first column of this chart to find out how much you already know:

1. Censorship of film.
2. Popular music and youth culture.
3. Charity advertising campaigns.
4. Politics and the media.
5. Far Eastern cinema.
6. Games consoles.
7. Children and television.
8. Radio news programmes.
9. Crime and the media.
10. Television makeover shows.
11. Auteur theory.
12. Digital video films.
13. Bollywood cinema.
14. Sport and the media.
15. Documentaries.
16. Representations of disability on television.
17. Narratives in TV soap operas.
18. Women and film.

| Media Topic: | Solo Activity: What I already know | Pair Activity: What I need to know more about |
|---|---|---|
| **What?** | | |
| **Who?** | | |
| **Where?** | | |
| **When?** | | |
| **Why?** | | |
| **How?** | | |

## PAIR/SMALL GROUP ACTIVITY

Now, work in a pair or small group and take it in turns to discuss what you have put in the first column. Use the second column to record what else you would need to research if you were able to choose this topic as a research topic.

## EXTENSION ACTIVITIES

1. Use a selection of newspapers to find your own key media issue. Share your findings with the class, using the WHAT? WHO? WHERE? WHEN? WHY? HOW? format.

2. Focus on a media institution, e.g. the BBC, Sony, Disney, Emap or Nintendo. Use the WHAT? WHO? WHERE? WHEN? WHY? HOW? format to gather enough information about the media institution to put together a wall display.

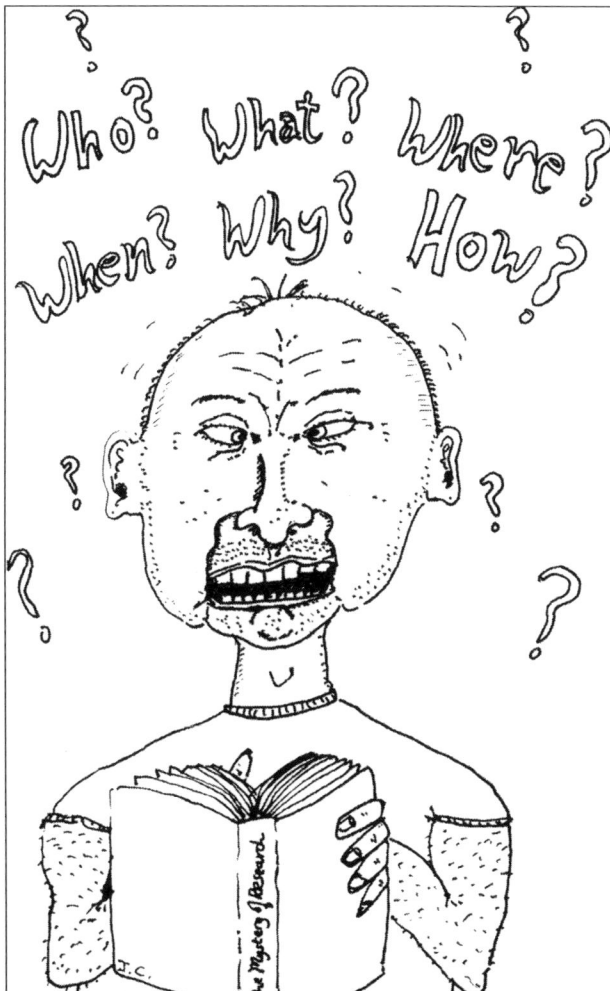

## TOP TIP

There is no right answer, but your research needs to demonstrate that you have thought about the question. Try to ask yourself these 6 key questions throughout your research.

**1.2**

# 1.2 FINDING IDEAS ON THE INTERNET

You will find the Internet to be a valuable source of ideas and information for your research work and, moreover, you will be using a form of the media to learn more about the media. Later sections in this pack will advise you on how to use the Internet safely and effectively. But, for now, let's see how Internet sites can offer you different viewpoints on a media issue:

1. Look at the BBC website, found at www.bbc.co.uk.

2. Choose a media issue, for example, music piracy.

3. Use the links to find articles representing different views on the issue, for instance, the attitude of artists such as David Bowie and Metallica; music industry perspectives, including the prosecution of those who illegally download large quantities of music; the opinions of audiences; new media developments, such as the iPod.

4. Print out a selection of articles which represent different viewpoints.

5. Complete this chart to compare what these different sources can offer the media researcher. Your evaluation of the source is important as it gives you an opportunity to be discriminating and not just accept it at face value. You may perhaps feel that the source is useful because it is balanced or has been written by someone with proven authority in this field or because it gives you an alternative approach. On the other hand, you may find weaknesses in the source if, for example, it offers unsupported opinions or it is biased or too dated.

| Source | Summary of the Source | Statistics/Data Quotes | Media Focus, e.g. Audience, Institutions, New Media Technology | Evaluation of Source |
|---|---|---|---|---|
| 1 | | | | |
| 2 | | | | |
| 3 | | | | |
| 4 | | | | |

6. Use this space to brainstorm possible research titles which use these 4 sources as a starting point.

7. Repeat the exercise, again using bbc.co.uk, but this time with a different topic.

## EXTENSION ACTIVITIES

1.  To find out more about the authority of one of your articles, apply the WHAT? WHO? WHERE? WHEN? WHY? HOW? rule to it.

2.  Write 500 words on the advantages and disadvantages of using the Internet for research, offering detailed examples.

## TOP TIP

Don't believe everything which jumps out of the Internet; check out the sources and authority of each site.

**1.3**

# 1.3 LOOKING AT EXISTING RESEARCH FOR IDEAS

## GROUP ACTIVITY

Below is a list of example research titles. Your syllabus may require you to carry out research in a different way, but it will be useful to consider possible research titles. Work through this first activity as a group, agreeing and sharing out tasks. You will need at least a facilitator, a scribe and a spokesperson to present your comments back to the class.

1. Decide on which research titles you think would be the most **easy** to do and why – label these **e**.

2. Agree on which you think would be the most **difficult** to do and why – label these **d**.

3. Discuss which you think would be the most **interesting** to do and why – label these **i**.

## TYPICAL EXAMPLES OF RESEARCH TITLES:

1. How are women who use violence represented in film? A comparative study of *Charlie's Angels* (2000), *Crouching Tiger, Hidden Dragon* (2000) and *Kill Bill: Volume 1* (2003).

2. A study of the representation of heroes and villains in the horror genre.

3. What the Hutton Report reveals about the relationship between politics and the media.

4. A comparison of the representation of disability in the films *My Left Foot* (1989), *The Station Agent* (2003) and *Inside I'm Dancing* (2004).

5. An investigation into the symbiotic relationship between sport and the media.

6. How is gender represented in advertising aimed at children and how do children respond to this representation?

7. An analysis of the representation of ethnic groups in two adventure films.

8. Why do women like chick flicks?: An investigation into female reception of romantic comedies.

9. A study of narrative form in TV hospital dramas.

10. An exploration of the notion of 'auteur' through one particular director.

11. Could we live without new media technologies? An investigation into audience consumption of new media technologies.

## TYPICAL EXAMPLES OF RESEARCH TITLES (cont.):

12. A study of the influence of cinema from the Far East.

13. A comparison of the representation of politics in a broadsheet and a tabloid newspaper.

14. A detailed investigation into the relationship between youth culture and controversial song lyrics.

15. Compare the remake of *Psycho* (1998), with the original (1960), with a focus on audience response.

16. An investigation into the resurgence of the documentary film, with particular reference to the following documentaries all released in 2004: *Fahrenheit 9/11*, *Super Size Me*, *The Corporation*.

17. A study of the use of narrative in TV evening news programmes.

18. Exploring genre codes and conventions: An analysis of comedy film trailers.

19. A comparison of narrative form in crime TV series and crime films.

20. Research into the representation of gender in television advertising.

Finally, you need to jot down notes in your Research Journey Record (see 4.4) – have these topics given you any ideas for your own research?

**1.3**

## EXTENSION ACTIVITIES

1.  From the list of 20 titles, pick the topic that appeals to you most and **make a list of 10 things** you would need to do to carry out research into it. You could then repeat this procedure for your final choice of topic, as approved by your teacher.

2.  Start to think of dynamic and snappy titles for research topics, e.g.

    'Ugh! I hate Barbie!': An investigation into how children respond to gendered advertising.

OR

    'Audiences like to see the forces of law and order triumph in crime TV series and to see the criminal triumph in crime films': A comparison of narrative form in crime TV series and crime films.

OR

    'Not just for kids': A study of the expanding audiences for animation films, with a particular focus on *Kirikou and the Sorceress* (1998), *Spirited Away* (2001) and *Belleville Rendez-Vous* (2003).

OR

    'It's a love/hate relationship': A comparison of the treatment of celebrities in *Hello!* and *heat* magazines.

---

### TOP TIP

If you have a choice, choose a topic which is manageable and which you will enjoy discussing, exploring and analysing.

---

## 1.4 TOPIC IDEAS

It can be very daunting to be asked to come up with your own research topic. You may be guided to focus on texts or issues or concepts. You may feel you know nothing about anything or you may be aware that your own beliefs and opinions could make it difficult to carry out objective research. This is when you need to seek the help of others. In fact, talking to other people will help you greatly with all aspects of your research and you could build this initial research into focus groups. At all times, you will need to be guided by your syllabus requirements.

## IDEA 1 – RESEARCH THE AUDIENCE

If there is a particular topic you are interested in, go and talk to the people who know something about this topic, for example:

1.  **Pop music and youth culture:** talk to a member of an older generation about the influence of pop music on them.

2.  **New media technologies:** find a selection of ages to talk to, from child to older person and ask questions to discover how much they use or know about new media technologies.

3.  **Women and film:** use a selection of film magazines to start off a discussion about how women are represented in film.

4.  **Children and TV:** observe how children use television and ask their parents what they have noticed about how their children use television.

5.  **Politics and the media:** notice the reactions of your family to party political broadcasts, war reporting, parliamentary debates and local politics.

6.  **Sport and the media:** ask family and friends about the advantages of interactive TV in sports coverage.

7.  **Community radio:** talk to family and friends who listen to local radio.

**1.4**

## IDEA 2 – RESEARCH THE INSTITUTIONS

Another approach is to put yourself in the place of media institutions and to ask yourself questions from their point of view. Most media institutions conduct audience research, and experience in this could be an advantage in seeking media employment. Media institutions might ask themselves some of the following questions:

1. What makes an effective charity advertising campaign?

2. How can music artists be transformed into a brand which can be marketed to audiences in different ways?

3. Is it possible to create a unisex lifestyle magazine?

4. How dependent are tabloid newspapers on their love/hate relationship with celebrities?

5. How easy is it to make a film with representations of strong and independent women?

6. Does television reflect the diverse groups within our society?

7. How do we incorporate new media technologies into our media products?

8. How do studios make use of the auteur concept?

## IDEA 3 – RECORDING YOUR IDEAS FOR POSSIBLE SOURCES

| MY POSSIBLE TOPICS, TEXTS, ISSUES, CONCEPTS | WHICH AUDIENCES AND / OR INSTITUTIONS COULD HELP ME? | HOW COULD THEY HELP ME? |
|---|---|---|
| | | |

## EXTENSION ACTIVITIES

1.  Play 'Ask the Expert' in class. Each student writes down a media topic on a piece of paper and puts it in a box. Take it in turns to pull out a piece of paper and say what you know about that topic.

2.  In pairs, choose a topic and devise **6 key questions** about that topic. Ask another pair if they can answer your questions.

---

### TOP TIP

Tell your family and friends what you plan to research as anyone who consumes the media will be able to give you some ideas.

---

**1.5**

# 1.5 THE STORY BEHIND THE HEADLINES

Study these invented headlines and, next to each, jot down possible research ideas. Then rank the headlines from 1 (easiest to research) to 12 (hardest to research).

| HEADLINE | POSSIBLE RESEARCH IDEAS | RANKING |
|---|---|---|
| Men steer clear of chick flicks. | | |
| Shocking charity campaign banned. | | |
| Text ads irritate phone users. | | |
| Why our kids need to ditch the TV | | |
| Far Eastern cinema leads the way. | | |
| Soaps slammed for sensational storylines. | | |
| Digital TV heralds 'free for all' for sports fans. | | |
| Group condemns crime films for glamorising serious issues. | | |
| Why we buy into the celebrity brand. | | |
| Growing concern at junk food advertising. | | |
| Special effects at the cinema: Why we can't get enough. | | |
| Less is more: How are independent films challenging the Hollywood blockbusters? | | |

## EXTENSION ACTIVITIES

1. For the topic you have ranked as '1', spend 10 minutes devising a mind map where you record all possible ideas on that topic.

2. Now use some of the newspaper sites recommended in the Webography to carry out a search of other headlines and articles which might be relevant to this topic.

## TOP TIP

Maintain a lively interest in what's going on in the media: read the media sections of newspapers and magazines, watch and listen to relevant TV and radio programmes, get used to discussing media issues with friends and family.

**1.6**

# 1.6 STARTING FROM A THEORETICAL PERSPECTIVE

In Media Studies and Film Studies, just as in any other academic discipline, there exists a body of knowledge and ideas known as **theory**. The theory may be specific to Media Studies and Film Studies or it may be applied across a range of academic disciplines. Theory consists of knowledge, ideas and approaches, which have been investigated and developed by specialists in their field. Your research will probably need to incorporate theory, because it will inform your work and demonstrate that you have considered the work of others. Your choice of research topic may stem from your interest in a particular theory or you may incorporate theory at a later stage.

There are many theoretical approaches which are relevant to Media Studies and Film Studies. Consult the Bibliography, your syllabus and your teacher for more information on theories. As a starting point, here is a simplified guide to the main features of some key theories, with examples of media texts which they could be applied to:

| THEORY | A MAIN FEATURE | COULD BE APPLIED TO... | RELEVANCE TO MY RESEARCH? |
|---|---|---|---|
| Feminism | Representation of women in the media. | Role of women as film-makers. | |
| Marxism | Critique of the dominance of the masses by a ruling class. | Advertising. | |
| Pluralism | Many media products made by many people for many audiences; we have a range of choices. | New media technologies. | |
| Postmodernism | Anything goes, anything can be challenged and everything is of equal value in a world where we create our own sense of reality. | Music videos. | |
| Semiotics | Study of signs. | Textual analysis of media texts. | |
| Structuralism | Narratives contain patterns. | TV crime dramas. | |

# 1.7 FINALISING YOUR RESEARCH PROPOSAL

Use this space to record your draft research proposal:

_____

_____

_____

_____

_____

_____

_____

_____

_____

_____

_____

_____

_____

_____

_____

Before you finalise your own research proposal, you need to be absolutely clear about what is required as different syllabuses have different rules. Using your syllabus and your teacher, answer the following questions (this will help to guide you towards a final research proposal):

1.  Does your syllabus have a limited choice of topics?

2.  Are you expected to use primary and/or secondary research?

3.  Do the media texts you are researching have to be contemporary?

4.  Are you required to focus just on textual analysis or can you incorporate audience and industry research?

5.  Is your idea for research appropriate for the key media concepts?

6.  Do you need to refer to wider relevant contexts?

7.  Does your research proposal seem manageable within the time allowed?

8.  Are you genuinely interested in your research proposal?

9.  Will you be able to find the resources and contacts you need to carry out this research?

10. Does your research proposal have a clear focus?

Now, consider what your final research proposal has to look like. For example:

## QUESTION:

How are children and young people represented in British TV soap operas?

## HYPOTHESIS:

Children and young people used to be rarely seen and rarely heard in British TV soap operas; this representation has had to change as soap producers seek younger audiences.

## DESCRIPTION:

A close study of the representations of children and young people in British TV soap operas.

## Use this space to record your final research proposal and check it with your teacher:

_____

_____

_____

_____

_____

_____

Now that you have a research proposal, you might find it helpful to complete the Research Proposal Form in Section 4.1. This will help you to start thinking about your chosen methodologies, which could include the following, depending on your syllabus requirements:

*textual analysis, content analysis, interviews, questionnaires, focus groups, secondary resource*

You may also need to consider whether **quantitative** or **qualitative** methods are most appropriate to your research.

| RESEARCH METHOD | SOME EXAMPLES | SOME FEATURES |
|---|---|---|
| Quantitative | Questionnaire; survey. | Data and statistics; large scale; describes trends; anonymity; tends to use what? when? where? questions. |
| Qualitative | Interview; focus group; case study; observation. | Quotations; small scale; focus on understanding and meanings; detailed; emphasis on point of view of participants; tends to use how? why? questions. |

# 2.1 ORGANISING YOUR RESEARCH

Effective research is well organised. There is a clear sense of purpose and direction; there is evidence of use of an appropriate range of sources and resources; and there are meaningful conclusions.

This is very much easier to do if you are organised about your research from the start. Setting up a system from the beginning gives you the opportunity to feel pleased about the way in which your work is building up and saves you extra work later on.

After discussion with your teacher concerning the requirements of your syllabus, consider the following list of suggestions for organising your research:

1. Card index file to record key ideas, references, etc.

2. Expanding file with several pockets to store different aspects of your research.

3. Ring binder with plastic wallets and dividers to sort and store information.

4. Small notebook which you can carry with you for interviews and jotting down ideas.

5. Research time chart with important targets and deadlines.

6. Separate files on your computer, saved in different ways to protect against loss.

7. Logbook or sheet to record every aspect of your research journey as it happens.

8. Time chart to remind you of important targets and deadlines.

9. Card folder for important documents and source material.

10. Separate files for primary and secondary research.

11. Computer files / floppies / digipen to store electronic information.

12. A3 mind map or Personal Digital Assistant to record all your ideas and feedback.

13. Box file to store bulkier items, e.g. DVD sleeves, video recordings, magazine pictures.

Now complete the chart overleaf.

**2.1**

| METHOD OF ORGANISATION | WHY I NEED IT AND HOW I WILL GET IT |
|---|---|
|  |  |

## EXTENSION ACTIVITIES

1.  Try using the number '3' as your guiding tool. Divide your main topic into 3 sections. divide each of these sections into 3, and so on. Some students find it helpful to have to work according to a tight structure like this.

2.  Get tips from someone who has experience of organising and storing large amounts of data and material as part of their job or study. Your teacher could perhaps advise you on how they manage all the data and material which forms part of their job.

### TOP TIP

Don't throw anything away as you don't know when you might need to return to an idea which you had earlier rejected.

# 2.2 MAKING THE MOST OF YOUR STRENGTHS

At this stage in your academic career, you should have a good awareness of your strengths. Carrying out research gives you the chance to evaluate your strengths and to make the most of them.

Complete the questionnaire below to remind yourself of your preferred learning styles.

## LEARNING STYLES QUESTIONNAIRE:

1. **I learn best through (number in order of preference):**

   ☐ Reading.

   ☐ Note-taking.

   ☐ Talking to people.

   ☐ Using technology, e.g. Internet, films.

   ☐ Drawing pictures and diagrams.

   ☐ Dealing with statistics and figures.

   ☐ Working on my own.

   ☐ Being physical and doing things.

2. **My best time for learning is (number in order of preference):**

   ☐ Morning.

   ☐ Afternoon.

   ☐ Evening.

   ☐ Night.

3. **I think my teachers would describe me as possessing the following skills (tick all those which apply):**

   ☐ Listening.

   ☐ Clear and articulate writing.

   ☐ Confidence in a small group.

   ☐ Confidence in a large group.

   ☐ An ability to consider all aspects of an issue.

   ☐ Originality.

   ☐ A methodical approach.

   ☐ Motivation.

   ☐ Attention to detail.

   ☐ Persistence.

   ☐ An enquiring mind.

   ☐ An ability to manage time well and to meet deadlines.

Now write 100 words identifying your strengths and how you think they will be used in your research work. You also need to consider your weaknesses and whether you will need to work at them to succeed with research.

**2.2**

## EXTENSION ACTIVITIES

1. Check your syllabus and make a list of what you need to do for your research. Match your learning style strengths to this list and begin with the task which makes best use of your strengths.

2. List your weaknesses and, with each, think of a way to overcome, avoid or re-direct it.

---

### TOP TIP

Allow this knowledge of your preferred learning styles and study skills to influence how you work, for example, by tackling the activity you find hardest when you are most alert and tackling easier activities such as making lists, watching relevant programmes and organising your work when you are tired or short of time.

---

# 2.3 DEVELOPING YOUR READING SKILLS

It goes without saying that reading skills are of vital importance when carrying out research. You will be reading several different types of document, from challenging academic material to magazine articles and emails. Each document will have its own codes and conventions. It is important not to be intimidated by what others have written, but to make a determined effort to understand and consider it.

**Here are some strategies you can follow to read and understand documents more fully:**

1.  Start by considering the author and what their likely standpoint is – this will help you to understand their point of view and who they're writing for.

2.  Always read actively and for a purpose.

3.  Read the first and last sentences of each paragraph, which should introduce and summarise the contents of the paragraph.

4.  Read a text, then make notes in two columns, one column supporting the ideas expressed in the text and the other column challenging them.

5.  Practise interpreting statistics, always being aware of the figures which are being given and those which are being left out.

6.  Use a dictionary to help you learn and apply new vocabulary.

7.  Note the date of the text: is it recent enough for you or is it a classic text which is still of some relevance?

8.  Check the position and authority of the writer by using the index to look up a subject with which you are familiar.

9.  'Furnish the mind' – read a page, then turn it over and recount what you've read, even if to yourself, as means of getting the information into your head.

10. Try to recall information the next day – talk to someone about what you read the day before or jot down 5 key points you remember from your reading.

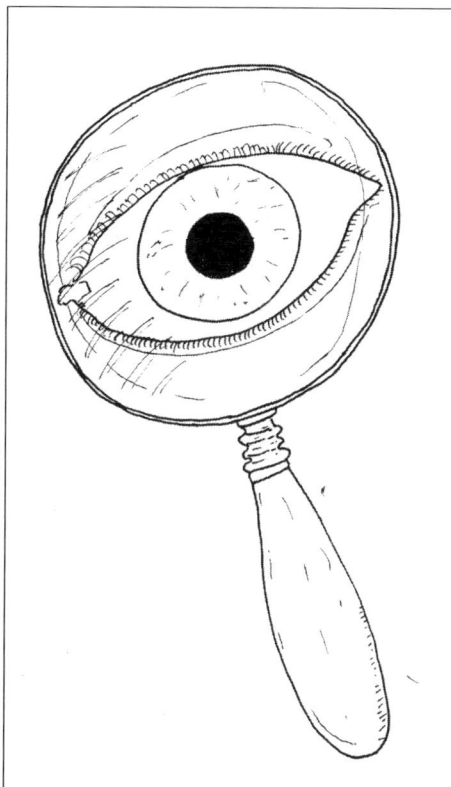

**The following suggestions might apply if the text is yours and you are free to write on it:**

1.  Read actively, for a purpose, and don't be afraid to annotate.

2.  Mark the margin with ticks, crosses and question marks to show where you agree, disagree or don't understand the points being made.

3.  Use coloured pens or highlighters to pick out different aspects of the text, for example, points for and against a particular argument.

4.  With a pen, draw a line through all the parts of the text which are of no use to you and highlight those parts which are useful – you need to exercise the powers of selection and rejection.

5.  Use the text as a model for your own writing, observing how the writer makes a point, provides evidence and then analyses it.

Finally, keep a record of the texts you consult: look at the Bibliography at the back of this pack or at the end of any academic text to find out about the accepted format for writing a bibliography.

Here are 3 texts to read in different ways as above – try out some of the above methods to discover which suits you:

## 1. EMAIL (a fictional example)

```
Dear Eleyna

Thank you for your email and I hope I can answer some of
your questions.

Our campaign group was set up in 1996 and is called
'Allowed to Be Children (ABC)'. Our mission is to campaign
against companies which we think encourage children to grow
up too quickly. I'm sure you can see this around you too,
that from comics and magazines through to fashion and music,
children are being treated as young adults, rather than
being allowed to enjoy being just children.

We disapprove of those pop stars who should be role models
to children but who instead are just fashion models,
encouraging their young fans to wear outfits which are not
appropriate for children. We think there should be more
regulation of the music industry with some artists and bands
having their lyrics censored if they are offensive. There
are far too many teenage girls' magazines around which
encourage their readers to think about nothing but sex.

What do you think about these issues? If you or your
parents would like to contact us, we would be delighted to
have you join our campaign.

Best wishes,

Stella,

Allowed to Be Children campaign (ABC)
```

## 2. MAGAZINE / NEWSPAPER WRITING (popular criticism)

From 'Soap bubble is near bursting', an article by David Liddiment, who was an Executive Producer of **Coronation Street** (*The Guardian*, 7 June, 2004, p. 5 of the Media supplement)

I don't know if you've noticed but there has been an extraordinary amount of *Coronation Street* about recently. Last week alone ITV transmitted seven episodes, three of them on the same night…

The *Coronation Street* lead-in has always been the most coveted on ITV, just as following *EastEnders* is the best slot on BBC1 to grow a hit – look at *Holby City* and *My Family*. And look, too, how the huge interest in the last ever episode of *Friends* gave Channel 4 the best possible launch pad for *Big Brother 5*…

And more episodes demand more stories which demand more cliffhangers to keep us hooked, and that means our credulity gets stretched more often. ITV1 and BBC1 have become addicted to soap… We are now almost at soap gridlock with both channels relying almost exclusively on the power of soap to maximise audience share, to support the rest of the schedule and to launch new programmes. It is no exaggeration to say that if Britain lost its appetite for soap, both BBC1 and ITV would collapse.

## 3. ACADEMIC WRITING

From *Dictionary of Media and Communication Studies* by James Watson and Anne Hill (2003)

### Crime: types of crime on screen

*Five types of on-screen crime are identified by Jessica Allen, Sonia Livingstone and Robert Reiner in an article 'True lies: changing images of crime in British postwar cinema', in the* European Journal of Communications, *March 1998. The authors surveyed 1461 crime-related films released between 1945 and 1991, and popular with the public, reporting that 'contrary to general beliefs about increased crime content of the media…our data shows a constant rate of representation, at least in the cinema over 50 years'.*

*The authors discuss primary, consequential, collateral and contextual crimes. To the first, that which animates the NARRATIVE, they ascribe the term McGUFFIN, borrowed from film director Alfred Hitchcock, 'to refer to the object whose pursuit provides the driving force of the narrative'. Consequential crimes are those that are committed in the course of, or in order to, cover up the McGuffin, while collateral crimes are not directly related to the McGuffin though they may be committed by the central criminals. Contextual crimes may also be unrelated to the McGuffin, the primary crime, 'but portray aspects of the wider society'.*

*Chief among McGuffins, say Allen, Livingstone and Reiner, is homicide, 48 per cent of their sample films having a homicide McGuffin – contrasting substantially with crime figures in the real world, where 90 per cent of recorded offences are property crimes. The authors noted an increase in contextual crimes during the 1960s: 'This is significant because it is contextual crime perhaps even more than the McGuffin which creates a sense of society as a whole being threatened by crime.'*

*This trend is linked to the 'increasing predominance of police heroes rather than amateur "sleuths"'; 'towards an increasingly graphic presentation of violence in the portrayal of crime'; the degree to which crime traumatises the victim, and the perception that crime has social origins. In their analysis, Allen, Livingstone and Reiner emphasise the complexity of the representation of crime in contexts of the 'collapse of moral certainties' in society, the dominance of Hollywood, the retreat from strict forms of CENSORSHIP and the demographic nature of AUDIENCE – largely made up of young people.*

## EXTENSION ACTIVITIES

1. Gather together and analyse 3 different types of writing required by your research.

2. Choose the most difficult text you have come across. Experiment with a range of reading strategies and then, after one week, judge which reading strategy has helped you to understand and retain the meaning of the text.

> **TOP TIP**
>
> Show respect for the experts, but be ready to challenge their work too.

# HOW TO FIND MEDIA STOCK IN A LIBRARY

As you will know if you have ever tried to find media stock in a library, it is rarely all in the same place.

Here are some suggestions for where you should be able to find useful media texts in a library based on the Dewey System. Remember also to look at non-print resources, e.g. CDs, DVDs, online libraries, databases and CD Roms. When in doubt, ask a librarian.

## BOOKS

| | |
|---|---|
| 51.82 | Magazines |
| 070 | Newspapers |
| 300.72 | Research Methods |
| 301 | Sociology |
| 302.23 | Media Studies |
| 302.23 | Advertising |
| 302.2322 | Newspapers |
| 302.2344 and 791.43 | TV, Radio and Film |
| 302.2345 and 791.45 | Television |
| 306 | Culture |
| 306 and 796 | Sport |
| 320 | Politics |
| 364 | Crime |
| 770 | Photography |
| 780 | Music |
| 791 | Films |

## REFERENCE

| | |
|---|---|
| 300 | 'Issues' series by Donnellan |
| 302.23 | *The Guardian Media Guide* |
| 781.63 | Popular Music Guides |
| 791.4 | *BFI Film and TV Handbook* |
| 791.43 | Film Guides |

## JOURNALS

*Creative Review*

*Empire Magazine*

*In the Picture*

*Media Magazine*

*Sight and Sound*

*Televisual*

## NEWSPAPERS

*The Guardian* (especially Monday's Media supplement)

*The Observer*

*The Sunday Times* (first issue of the month currently carries a free CD with media resources)

## EXTENSION ACTIVITIES

1. Use 3 different sources to find out more about your topic.

2. Cross off the sources you have consulted before and have a look at those which are new to you.

## TOP TIP

Always record the full reference of any book, article or website you consult; it can be hard work trying to find it later.

**2.4**

# 2.4 WORKING ON YOUR TALKING AND LISTENING SKILLS

Your research will probably require you to talk to people to gain any information you might need from audiences, institutions and producers. You need to take advice from your teacher on who you should approach and the safety guidelines you should follow to protect yourself.

You need to think about how to talk to different people to get the information you need. You need to be well prepared yet flexible enough to realise when to adapt your talking to accommodate new ideas. Your research topic and the nature of your interviewees will guide you in terms of how structured or unstructured you want the interviews to be.

When talking to people for research purposes, the key ideas you need to bear in mind are **full and informed consent** and **avoidance of harm**. Talking to people can be done in a variety of ways as shown below:

## Interviews

1. Obtain full and proper consent by designing your own consent form for participants and/or their parents/ guardians. You have a responsibility to inform interviewees what the interview will ask of them; what the information they give you will be used for and that they have a right not to answer questions and to end the interview whenever they wish. You should inform them that they have a right to confidentiality and a right not to be identified, except perhaps by their age and gender. You also need to consider whether interviewees might wish to see a transcript of their interview or the entire work when it is finished.

2. Be polite – someone has given up their time to talk to you, so show good manners, letting them know at the beginning how long the interview will last, thanking them at the end and generally making them feel safe and comfortable in the interview situation.

3. Before each interview, design a chart with the 6 key questions (who, what, why, etc.) and fill it in as soon as possible after the interview so you have a clear record of what happened in the interview.

4. Interviews generally offer qualitative data, giving you data in the form of quotations rather than statistics.

5. You may want to use stimulus material, e.g. DVD sleeves, song lyrics, magazine images or short film clips to get the conversation going.

6. Practise interviewing skills and ask for feedback on your talking and listening style before you start. Consider the importance of matters like location and seating.

7. Acknowledge that you can't listen, talk and take notes all at the same time – bring along a friend to take notes or a tape or voice recorder.

8. Plan your prompt questions carefully, so that the talk doesn't dry up and you don't dominate: you want to make it easy for your interviewees to contribute and to develop their answers.

9. Have a sense of where you want the interview to go, but learn to accommodate extra comments or directions which emerge. If your interviewee seems to be wandering off the point, look for constructive ways in which you can return to your question.

10. If you're not clear about something which is said, ask the interviewee to repeat it or rephrase it until you understand fully: remember to check the interviewee has a full understanding of your question.

11. Remember to ask your interviewee at the end if there is anything else they wish to add and to thank them for their time.

## ACTIVITY – GROUPS OF 3

Practise your interviewing skills, choosing your own research topic or one from the following list. Work in groups of 3, where one person interviews a second person and the third person observes and gives feedback. Continue, changing roles each time.

1. Influence of TV on boys' and girls' attitudes and behaviour.

2. Representation of different social groups in soap operas.

3. Role of children in magazine advertising.

4. Programming in community radio.

5. Representations of disability on TV.

6. Benefits of interactive TV.

7. Music and subcultures.

8. Self-regulation in the press.

9. Reality television.

10. Music videos: Art or advert?

11. Female film directors.

12. Influence of Japanese animation.

13. Big budget versus low budget films.

14. The rise of the documentary.

15. Censorship and the cinema.

16. Popularity of film remakes.

### Focus Groups

1. Focus groups offer you the chance to gain information from a small number of people at the same time.

2. In many ways, they are similar to interviews, but you have the added dynamic of what goes on in groups, which is that people debate and interact with each other, changing their minds and changing other people's minds.

3. Explain to your focus group what will happen, how much of their time you will need and why you have set up a focus group.

4. Focus groups are regularly used by media industries, so experience in running one could be good preparation for employment in media research.

5. In a focus group, your role will be as a facilitator, prompting group discussion with questions and making sure that everyone has a chance to have a say.

6. Ideally, you need to prepare a stimulus to start off discussion, for example, a collection of tabloid reports of celebrities; extracts from films directed by women; examples of interactive websites; a selection of children's television programmes; print, broadcast and film coverage of one type of crime; extracts from the work of an auteur.

7. The size of your group needs to be large enough to get a good discussion going, but not so large that people have to shout to be heard.

8. As with interviews, keep a record of who your participants are and use a friend/tape or voice recorder/video camera to record key ideas and quotations.

9. Remember to evaluate your focus group – what information did it give you and what else will you need to do to plug the gaps for any missing information?

10. Consider carefully whether you can generalise from the findings of your focus group, or whether your findings are relevant to that group only.

## ACTIVITY

In small groups take it in turns to plan and conduct a focus group on one aspect of your research. Focus groups normally run for one hour maximum, but 15–20 minutes each in class should give you a good idea of how to run a focus group and what it feels like to be in one.

## Observation

You may like to consider observation as a methodological tool, where you watch and observe audiences using the media. Observation may appeal to you because it seems more natural and less constructed. This may be particularly so with children, who could reveal more information as they are watching the TV, rather than being asked formal questions about their viewing habits and preferences. Remember, any research, particularly that concerned with children, should show that you have obtained **full and informed consent** (from children and parents/guardians) and that you have given due thought to an **avoidance of harm**.

Again, you must keep records of what happens. You also need to decide in advance whether you have a set of observable behaviours you are going to look for and mark up a grid in advance or whether you will observe what's there and analyse afterwards.

Observations can be very rewarding because you never quite know what is going to happen. This can be a disadvantage, too, as you have to be prepared for the possibility that observations will not provide the information you need.

One variation of observation is called 'participant observation' where you join in the activity yourself and note down your observations afterwards; an example of this could be going to the cinema and observing the nature and behaviour of audiences for a romantic comedy film.

## ACTIVITY

How you carry out this activity will depend on who you can observe. If you are on a work placement in a school or nursery, for example, you could observe children watching schools programming on TV or in a computing lesson. As a babysitter or older brother or sister, you could observe the ways in which young children watch TV at home. You could observe how an older generation watches and comments on the news or crime programmes or you could explore the relationship between sport and the media by observing how audiences make use of interactive technologies when watching sport on TV. Make the most of your opportunities.

When you come back to class, report what you have learned about the advantages and disadvantages of the observational approach.

**2.4**

## EXTENSION ACTIVITIES

1. Watch television interviews to acquire techniques for talking to people.

2. Copy and complete this chart so you can compare different approaches.

| METHOD | ADVANTAGES | DISADVANTAGES | WILL I USE THIS METHOD? |
|---|---|---|---|
| Observation | | | |
| Focus group | | | |
| Interviews | | | |
| Questionnaires | | | |
| Other… | | | |

**TOP TIP**

Pilot your questionnaires and interview questions first, so you can then modify them.

# 2.5 QUESTIONNAIRES

1.  Consider their purpose: will they act as a useful first step to help you identify interviewees for later?

2.  What other methodologies will you use? Questionnaires on their own may not be adequate for A2 research, so check your syllabus demands.

3.  What will they offer you? If it is purely data, you will need a high number of respondents for this to be worthwhile. You can represent this data mathematically, via fractions or percentages, graphs or charts. The data can also provide a useful bank of statistics and quotations for your report if your syllabus allows this.

4.  You need some kind of identification on each form, perhaps by numbering each one or by indicating the age or gender of the respondent.

5.  Pilot it on yourself and on friends so you can work on the difficult questions and adapt them if needed.

6.  Draw your respondent in by making the questions easy to answer, particularly at the beginning, and using a variety of questioning styles, such as True / False statements, lists to prioritise or numbers to circle ranking from 1 to 5. You could offer trigger sentences to complete or ask for an opinion by writing out an open question.

7.  Check whether your questions are open or closed and that they are clear and not opinionated.

## ACTIVITY

In small groups, find the errors in the questions below and rewrite them so they are more effective:

1.  Do you believe that *EastEnders* is the best soap on TV and that *Emmerdale* is rubbish? Please answer YES or NO.

2.  People have often said that Quentin Tarantino is the best director around and I agree because all his films are great. How do you rate him as a director, on a scale of 0 to 30?

3.  Do young people aged 16–25 read any newspapers? Answer YES, NO or DON'T KNOW.

## EXTENSION ACTIVITIES

1.  Have fun making up some more questions with errors in them, then pass them round the class for others to rewrite.

2.  Study questionnaires from magazines and other sources to identify the strategies used to acquire information.

## TOP TIP

Try not to influence your respondents into giving you the answer you want them to give you. Being open-minded will give you more to think about for your research.

**2.6**

# 2.6 PRIMARY AND SECONDARY RESEARCH

**Primary research** is that which is carried out entirely by you. Check your syllabus as it may only allow you to carry out primary research in the form of textual analysis. In Media Studies and Film Studies, primary research is generally divided into two types:

*(i) Talking to people*, through methods such as observation, interviews, case studies, questionnaires and focus groups. People you talk to could be audiences or from media industries.

*(ii) Textual analysis*, where you analyse and show your own understanding of media texts, for example, through content or semiotic analysis. A Media Studies or Film Studies course gives you plenty of practice in textual analysis, so draw on this experience.

Primary research gives you the chance to explore something in a way which has never been done before; primary research is what makes your research unique. You will need to balance your primary research with secondary research to show you have considered the views and expertise of others.

**Secondary research** consists of work that someone else has done which you consider and refer to. Does your research fit in with existing research, challenge it or develop it in some way? Have you taken cultural contexts, media theories and key concepts into account?

Secondary research can take a range of forms: academic articles and studies; popular criticism, as in magazine and newspaper articles; websites; TV programmes; DVDs; videos; films; radio programmes.

Remember to reflect on and evaluate your secondary research sources, demonstrating that you can engage with them.

## ACTIVITY

To help you compare what different sources can offer, it's often useful to explore their different perspectives on the same topic. Analyse the following pieces of writing, which are all on the topic of soap operas and find out what you can about the author, publication and target audience of each. This will then help you to place your secondary research into some kind of context.

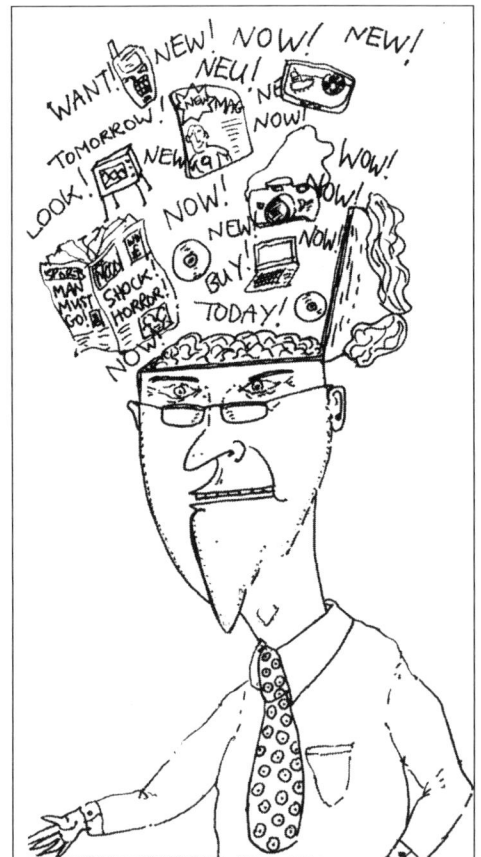

**TOP TIP**

Adopt an hour glass approach: begin by gathering plenty of background material for your topic, then narrow it down by selecting the most important elements, then explore those elements in some depth.

## Source 1: 'Soap bubble is near bursting'

*ITV1 and BBC1 have become addicted to soap. I understand how we got here, but I can't help thinking it's not a healthy place to be, both for the channels and the soaps themselves. We are now almost at soap gridlock with both channels relying almost exclusively on the power of soap to maximise audience share, to support the rest of the schedule and to launch new programmes. It is no exaggeration to say that if Britain lost its appetite for soap, both BBC1 and ITV1 would collapse.*

(David Liddiment, once an executive producer of **Coronation Street**, writing in *The Guardian*, 7 June 2004)

## Source 2: 'Soap opera plots'

*Soap operas are 'open' texts, unlike most narratives which are said to be 'closed'. An open text is one allowing multiple interpretations. Open texts such as soap operas contain many characters and therefore points of view. There is usually no single hero. Characters often experience changes. The plot is rarely resolved. Any resolution is simply to allow for the next conflict.*

(extract from Chapter 4 of *Media and Meaning*, 2001 )

## Source 3: 'The search for tomorrow in today's soap operas'

*Another way in which soap opera stimulates women's desire for connectedness is through the constant, claustrophobic use of close-up shots. Often only the audience is privileged to witness the characters' expressions, which are complex and intricately coded, signifying triumph, bitterness, despair, confusion – the entire emotional register, in fact.*

(Tania Modleski, 1982)

## Source 4: 'Fantasy island? (*Balamory*, the pre-school soap)'

*'It is an aspirational place, and very safe – but it isn't Toytown. There are real issues and problems – people sneeze, cough and fall over, they go to the dentist, they have allergies, there's a birth (baby girl) and there's even a death – one of Edie McCredie's (the Balamory minibus driver) friends has a cat that dies.*

*'You could say the show is unreal in that the sense of community we portray doesn't exist in a lot of places today.'*

(Brian Jameson, creator and producer of **Balamory**, interviewed for the *Radio Times*, 26 April–2 May 2003)

## Source 5: 'Publicity office for *EastEnders*'

*'We work with print media, television, radio and the internet. We plan ahead with magazines to tie features in with major storylines. For nine to twelve weeks in advance we'll be dealing with the long-lead magazines such as* Cosmopolitan. *We read all the* EastEnders *scripts and send out story highlights to the* EastEnders *website and all the listings magazines about seven weeks in advance. This allows everyone to plan their covers and interviews.*

*As major storylines draw nearer, we work with the shorter lead media, such as national newspapers, TV and radio. We give them exclusive pictures of stories the week before a storyline actually happens. By the time that a storyline peaks, people should be aware that this week is the week to watch EastEnders. We want the public to know about the show, but we don't want to spoil their enjoyment by giving too much away.*

*The TV listings magazines are very important as they tell their readers what to look out for in the programme. To have EastEnders on all the covers of those magazines is a real achievement. Soap magazine covers are free advertising for the programme. Even if someone doesn't buy a magazine, they'll see someone from EastEnders grinning back at them from the shelf!'*

(Assistant Publicist Kirsty Wilson writing on the **EastEnders** website on www.bbc.co.uk/eastenders, posted on 8 July 2004)

## Source 6: 'Corrie comes out of the closet'

*'People always ask why it's taken 42 years,' says the scriptwriter Daran Little. 'But the gay content has always been implicitly there.' Bruno Langley, who plays Todd, says Corrie's coming out was inevitable. 'Manchester has a very big gay community. If Coronation Street doesn't at least nod to that, then it stops being about Manchester.' Little agrees: 'You have to be a mirror to the real world. If you don't then you run the risk of becoming outdated.'*

(Paul Flynn, writing in *The Guardian*, 1 March 2004)

# 2.7 INTERNET RESEARCH

The Internet offers a fantastic range of knowledge, most of which is free. It has also enabled the ordinary person to gain access to material much more easily, BUT you have to know how to use it efficiently. Where possible, check the identity, authority and background of Internet contributors – look at the site address, find out who they're writing for and what else they may have published, whether in a book or on the Internet. When in doubt, ask your teacher to check out the authority of the writer.

Remember also to observe Health and Safety guidelines, including keeping safe on the Internet and taking regular breaks from working with computers.

### How to find what you want

- To discover what different search engines can offer, try searching for the same topic using the following search engines:

  *altavista.co.uk*     *ask.co.uk*     *google.co.uk*     *hotbot.com*     *teoma.com*     *yahoo.co.uk*

- Check the country of origin, particularly if your syllabus has a requirement for British texts.

- Allow your choice of sites to be guided by the information you want to find: Data? Opinions? Academic research? Media industry statistics?

- Experiment with different combinations of key words and remember that putting in lots of key words will narrow your search down, whereas putting in one or two key words will open your research up.

### Web addresses and what they mean

.ac.uk – academic institution     .co.uk – British company     .com – worldwide company

.gov.uk – British government     .int – international     .org.uk – non-profit-making organisation

### How to find out about the author

• Look at the site address, its URL (Unique Reference Locator). • Are they an established name? • What else have they written? • Who are they writing for? • Links on site to anything else they've done? • Look at the language and tone: if it seems emotional, personal and overbearing, can you be sure you're reading a balanced, informed and intelligent article, if this is what you're looking for? • Check the date – you need a record of when you accessed the site and you need to know how recent and up to date it is.

### How to reference it

- As with any text, the 3 key references you need are the name of the person who wrote it, the title of the piece and the date when it was written.

- If these details aren't immediately obvious on the site, try looking in 'View' then 'Source' on the toolbar and work your way through the HTML script.

- You should also add the name of the site.

- As the Internet is subject to copyright like any other text, you must be sure to reference it.

## EXTENSION ACTIVITIES

1. Pick a media topic and choose 3 different sites to discover information on it, one academic, one broadcasting and one popular criticism. Compare the different approaches and information given.

2. Now cut and paste information from each of these sites into a new document where you omit any details of the source. Swap with someone else and see if you can detect which site is academic in origin, which is to do with broadcasting and which is popular criticism.

---

### TOP TIP

Try to find out a lot about one thing rather than not very much about lots of things.

---

**2.8**

## 2.8 PRESENTING A PROGRESS REPORT

Use this page to plan a progress report on your research, which you will give to the rest of your class. The progress report could:

1. Enable others to give you further help.

2. Provide a Key Skills Communication opportunity.

3. Give you the chance to learn more about the research of others.

4. Help you prepare for an assessed presentation to your peers.

You may want to use a range of resources while presenting your progress report: you could screen some of the film clips you have been analysing or use Powerpoint or an interactive whiteboard to show images and ICT links. While giving your progress report, it may be useful to ask a fellow student to jot down any interesting comments which are made, so you can incorporate them into your research also.

*...and this just in...*

| NAME | |
|------|------|
| **RESEARCH TOPIC** | |
| **PROGRESS I HAVE MADE SO FAR** | |
| **I STILL NEED HELP WITH** | |

## EXTENSION ACTIVITIES

1. Once you have your feedback from the class, set new targets and deadlines – there should be fewer now!

2. If you're feeling really brave, ask someone in the class to challenge your research and search out the weaknesses. It may seem like a scary experience to put yourself through, but it's better if you detect any weaknesses before an examiner does!

### TOP TIP

When taking a break, some researchers stop when they are in the middle of something which is going well; that way, they feel positive about the work and feel more inclined to return to it after a break.

## 3.1 EVALUATING RESEARCH

How do we know if a finished piece of research is any good or just long and obscure? Your teacher, syllabus and mark scheme will indicate the assessment objectives of your exam board and these exercises will help you evaluate your own work.

## ACTIVITY A

Read through the following possible indicators of quality in writing research and add 5 more of your own.

**Good research has:**

1. Plenty of supporting evidence.

2. A wide range of appropriate sources and references.

3. An interesting and enthusiastic style.

4. A clear framework.

5. A good choice of appropriate methodologies.

6. An intelligent and thorough style.

7. Evidence of close and logical analysis.

8. No unsupported assertions.

9. A strong and independent focus without generalisation.

10. Appropriate conclusions.

11. _____

12. _____

13. _____

14. _____

15. _____

## ACTIVITY B

Now you have established your criteria for success, have a look at these extracts, which are typical of student research in progress. Annotate each extract with the advice you would give to students at this stage in their research: what are they doing well and what areas do they need to work on?

## Student 1

My questionnaire for parents reflected how parents feel about television advertising aimed at children, and opinions do seem to vary greatly. Just 20% of the parents I questioned would support a total ban on television advertising aimed at children, claiming they 'would prefer to be able to choose what my child wants, rather than being told what they should have through the television'; yet 10% of these parents would not change anything about television advertisements aimed at children, saying 'I'm sure that they have no huge effect. Children are always going to want things, whether they've seen them on the television or not!' The remaining 70% of parents would welcome a ban on some advertisements, but felt it would not be essential to ban them all. If forced to ban one particular type of children's advertisements, the majority (90%) of the parents chose junk food, as they feel that this causes the most harm to their children. A complete ban may seem like a good plan to rid of 'pester power' and lower the risks of child obesity. However, the advertising industry has insisted that there is no correlation between food advertising and obesity (source: BBC News) ...Overall, I do not think that television advertisements are the only thing to blame for rising levels of obesity in children, however, they may have played a role in the popularity of certain junk foods. Advertisements have a huge amount of power, and 'pester power' is a pain for most parents.

## Student 2

The nature of the media means that the truth and politics are often forgotten when trying to gain an audience, especially in print-based media, so the more extremist the headline, the greater the readership.

## Student 3

A large centre of my work, I felt, should be based around work on existing theorists, and, in order to discover relevant academics to my research, I conducted a search on the popular Internet search engine entitled 'Google'. This led me to a wider knowledge of the topic I was investigating, thus enabling me to specify the result I desired from the study.

## Student 4

Whereas Dick Hebdige mainly discusses and emphasises the function of youth subcultures in constructing an identity that gives young people relative autonomy within an existing social order, based on my own findings I came to another conclusion. Punk and New Wave culture seemed to have been more than a fading style or fashion; more than something that was solely expressed by wearing certain clothes or listening to certain records. In fact, with people becoming active themselves, trying different things and attempting to live their lives to the extreme, regardless of what everyone else thought of them, Punk and New Wave seems to have been rather an ideology. It gave them something to hold on to in life and offered them the advice and answers they were looking for; as well as providing young people with a feeling of being part of a movement and belonging to a community of people who thought in the same ways as they did.

## Student 5

In horror, if the main part is a female, she is smart, pretty, young and thin. But if a woman plays the killer, she is either old or fat or unattractive (**Misery** (1990) and **Friday the 13th** (1980)). In romances, if the woman is unwanted as she appears less attractive than the average Hollywood actress, it is made clear that this is the reason. However, if the role is played by a very attractive woman, it is made clear that the reason is something else like her intelligence (**Legally Blonde** (2001)). Films give a definite stereotypical way a woman should look, and in films where they try to make women viewers feel more confident, they put the idea into our heads that at the end of it, all you do have to be is thin and pretty.

**3.1**

## EXTENSION ACTIVITIES

1.  Skim read your own piece of research 15 times, one for each of the 15 quality criteria you identified in Activity A.

2.  In your class, pass round each other's research and add helpful comments according to the 15 quality criteria statements.

---

### TOP TIP

Don't be too hard on yourself: all researchers will come up against problems and you need to demonstrate how you can work your way around them.

# 3.2 EVALUATION BY OTHERS

You may think your research will be seen only by you, your teacher and the examiner, but you should consider making your research available to a wider audience. This has several advantages: the possibility of further feedback; practice in presenting your research in different ways to different readers; it adds to the portfolio of your work which you can talk about at university and career interviews; and there is sometimes the possibility of publication!

Consider trying out one of the following ideas:

1.  Get together with others in your class and each write an account of your research in no more than 500 words. Put all of these accounts in a photocopied booklet and learn from each other. If your school or college has an intranet or suitable ICT facility, your work could be uploaded for others to access electronically.

2.  Offer to give a brief presentation to a younger class which outlines how to succeed at research, using your study as an example! Your presentation could be in any format, e.g. Powerpoint; OHP; Question and Answer.

3.  Write a summary of your research in 100 words. Send this summary to your school or college magazine / radio station and offer to be interviewed about it or to write it up for them.

4.  Consider a wider audience still. Look at your local paper to see if your material could be transformed into a brief column which might be of interest to the general reader. You will need to follow the newspaper's guidelines, but this is good experience in adapting your material for different audiences.

5.  *The Media Magazine* (published by The English and Media Centre) has expressed an interest in contributions by students.

Now you are on the research journey, don't end it there! You could continue this research at a higher level or it may have inspired you to carry out research into new topics.

## EXTENSION ACTIVITIES

1.  Show your research journey through pictures, e.g. as a cartoon or display which can then be used to advise and encourage future media students.

2.  Write a 50 word book blurb for your research, highlighting the main features.

---

**TOP TIP**

Sharing your research is good for you and good for others.

**3.3**

# 3.3 STRUCTURING YOUR MATERIAL

The way you organise your research depends on the format in which it will be assessed and you must seek guidance from your teacher and your syllabus on this. Using a word-processor to organise and edit your work is invaluable: even if you are required to write up your research in an exam situation, the use of a word-processor beforehand can help you to see the shape your written research could take.

## Overall structure

In an exam, you will have a specific question or questions to answer. For a coursework assignment, you may have been given a title or you may have had to make up your own title / hypothesis / argument / research question / brief.

If it is left completely up to you, you might like to follow one of the accepted forms for writing up research, as described here; check if headings are required or not:

- Background.

- Aims.

- Methods.

- Analysis of results.

- Conclusions.

## Paragraph structure

For your research to be graded as clear and fluent, you need to pay attention to how you write your paragraphs.

Your opening paragraph needs to be strong as it is the first impression you give of yourself to the examiner. Make sure it's clear, engaging and offers an accurate introduction to what will come later. Your closing paragraph also needs to be strong as it is the impression of yourself you leave the examiner with. It should contain an accurate and thoughtful summing-up of your research, perhaps ending on a quotation or interesting idea to provoke further thought.

Paragraphs within the body of your writing need attention too. To make your writing fluent, the opening sentence of each paragraph could link in some way to the closing sentence of the preceding paragraph. The opening sentence of each paragraph could also offer an accurate and interesting introduction and should signpost the ideas which will be developed within that paragraph; someone wishing to skim-read your research should be able to gain a fair idea of what it is about simply through reading the first sentence of each paragraph.

## Internal paragraph structure

Your research will have given you plenty of evidence to support your ideas. Show this by adopting the following 3-point structure:

1.  Make a point.

2.  Support it with evidence.

3.  Analyse it / incorporate theory.

Supporting your points with evidence and then analysing them and drawing in theory helps you towards the higher grades. Here is an example of the 3-point structure:

(i) Audiences are increasingly familiar with the codes and conventions of genre films and this is also to the advantage of institutions, which can repeat a winning formula. To prevent tedious repetition, audiences of genre films are frequently offered variations on a theme.

(ii) One example of audiences being offered 'the same but different' can be found in sequels such as **Speed 2: Cruise Control** (1997), which is located on a cruise ship instead of the bus which featured in **Speed** (1994).

(iii) Stephen Neale summarised this when he argued that genre films 'are processes articulated within a precise economy of repetition and difference' (Neale, 1980). We can therefore speculate that the combination of continuity and variety is a winning formula for both producers and audiences of genre films.

## EXTENSION ACTIVITIES

1.  Practise writing strong opening and closing statements for your research.

2.  Draw attention to longer quotations, statistics and data through indenting text, using bold, etc.

### TOP TIP

Try dividing your research into 3 parts, divide each of them into a further 3 parts, and so on. This method of organising research works really well for some people.

**3.4**

# 3.4 FORMAL CONVENTIONS OF PRESENTING RESEARCH

Consider these guidelines for some of the formal conventions of presenting research, then look at the examples below:

1.  Choose a title which is both catchy and informative – try using a quotation or question, lyric or headline.

2.  Set out long quotations separately.

3.  Know how to write a bibliography.

4.  Subjective ('I gathered information…') or objective ('Information was gathered…') style?

5.  Use of an appendix or appendices for attaching extra material at the end.

6.  Within your text, know how to put in references after quotations (name of author and date, with full reference in the bibliography).

7.  Use appropriate academic and media-specific language.

## EXTENSION ACTIVITIES

1.  Rewrite these sentences using the last point above (appropriate media terminology and analytical language):

    *   *The camera moves round and follows her up as she runs up the steps after the suspect, and then some cheesy music kicks in and we somehow know that she will catch him.*

    *   *This magazine has got loads of pictures in it and they all give a really bad impression of celebrities. What writing there is seems to shout in your face.*

    *   *I carried out several kinds of research, some worked and some didn't. I don't know why so many people said they were against this type of music as I think it's really good, but I suppose we can all make our own choices. People should be able to tell what they're going to get from the CD cover and it's up to them whether they buy it or not, I think.*

    *   *I think this director could definitely be categorised as an auteur because all his films are from the same genre and he always uses the same actors.*

2.  Ask your teacher or a librarian to find some examples of higher level research, perhaps university level, and see if you can identify some of the above formal conventions of academic research language.

> ## TOP TIP
>
> Demonstrate that your work has authority as a piece of media research through your confident use of media and research terminology.

# 3.5 THE FINAL CHECKLIST

So, you think you've finished? Research involves you working independently under supervision and this final checklist is an opportunity to evaluate everything you have done so far. Work your way through this checklist, ticking off what you've done and seeing what else you might need to do:

❏ Is your research appropriate for your syllabus requirements?

❏ Have you acted on the advice given to you by your teachers?

❏ Have you shown awareness of the cultural sensitivities of your participants?

❏ Check against your syllabus criteria that you have written in the style required, whether investigative research or an analytical essay.

❏ Does your research have a specific focus, while allowing you to demonstrate a breadth of knowledge about the topic as a whole?

❏ Does your research have an engaging title and does it sustain a reader's interest? Would you want to read it?

❏ Have you observed research ethics and Health and Safety issues?

❏ If you are allowed to take notes into the exam room, how good are they? Check again to see what you are allowed to do and get your teachers to check your notes too. Have you organised and colour coded them in such a way as to work to your benefit in the exam room?

❏ Have you forwarded attachments of your research to anyone who might be interested in giving you feedback or publishing it?

❏ Do you have evidence that you 'reflect' and 'evaluate'? Have you said how your research could have been made better if you were able to do it again? What are you proud of? What did you find out?

❏ Do you summarise your range of research methods?

❏ Does it sound like you know what you're talking about?

❏ Have you checked your work for inaccuracies?

❏ Do you make confident use of correct media terminology?

❏ If this is a synoptic unit, have you drawn together the key concepts and ideas you have learned in the course?

❏ Have you proofread? Are your points clear?

❏ Do you use theory with confidence?

❏ Do you demonstrate accurate and thorough research by referring to statistics and key dates?

❏ Is it a piece of independent research?

❏ Three-point structure – are each of your points backed up with textual evidence, analysis and is theory present?

❏ Have you kept detailed notes of all your sources? Is your bibliography of research resources full and complete?

❏ Have you checked against the grade criteria to see what you need to do to get the grade you want?

☐ Are there any gaps in your research? Have you covered all the requirements of primary, secondary, academic, institutional and popular research or whatever is mentioned in your syllabus?

☐ If required, have you used a personal voice ('I') to demonstrate your sense of delight, engagement, discovery and curiosity – if you have chosen your own research subject, you should be interested in it!

☐ As in advertising, is your research 'legal, decent, honest and truthful'?

☐ Define any key terms you use and the scope of your study.

☐ Does your research prove that you have carried out an investigation into a body of evidence, rather than taken an opportunity to give unsubstantiated opinion?

☐ Is your research reliable? (Would the results be the same if you did it again?) And is it valid? (Are the methods you chose honest and accurate? Was it the right approach?)

☐ Have you been careful not to plagiarise the work of others?

☐ Have you met the word count guidance or are you confident you can write everything you need to in an exam situation?

☐ Are you able to write a great opening and a great conclusion which will persuade the examiner you are worthy of a high mark?

☐ Do you provide plenty of details and supporting evidence?

☐ Does your study reflect, evaluate, show engagement with the work of others and demonstrate a fresh, personal and discriminating response?

☐ Does your conclusion answer the question you set yourself at the beginning?

☐ Do you promote yourself and show what you are proud of in your research?

If you've achieved all that, you have made a **superheroic** effort!

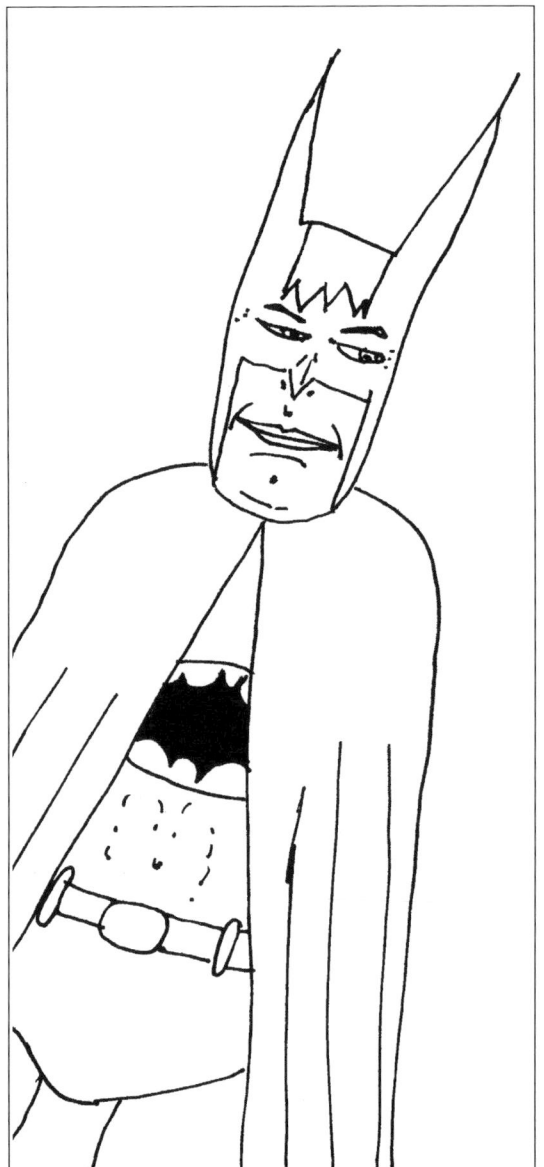

# 4.1 RESEARCH PROPOSAL FORM

Once you have decided on your research topic, fill in this form and ask your teacher to check it for you.

| **MY NAME** | |
|---|---|
| **WHAT?**<br>What do I want to research? | |
| **WHO?**<br>Who will I need to contact? | |
| **WHERE?**<br>Where will I find my information? | |
| **WHEN?**<br>When will I carry out this research? | |
| **WHY?**<br>Why is this topic worth researching? | |
| **HOW?**<br>How do I plan to carry out this research? | |

**4.2**

## 4.2 ACTION PLAN

Start by listing here everything you are required to do by your syllabus, e.g. textual analysis; audience research; secondary research; theoretical concepts; institutional research.

Now use this information to complete the chart below. The ACTION column will describe the individual actions you need to take, for example, creating a proposal or problematic; a textual analysis of a music video; a focus group watching animation clips; or researching theoretical studies of the thriller genre.

| DATE | ACTION | HOW THIS FITS INTO MY SYLLABUS REQUIREMENTS |
|------|--------|---------------------------------------------|
|      |        |                                             |

## 4.3 RECORD OF DEADLINES

| DATE OF DISCUSSION | AGREED TARGET – WHAT NEEDS DOING AND BY WHEN | STUDENT SIGNATURE | STAFF SIGNATURE |
|---|---|---|---|
| | | | |

**4.4**

# 4.4 A RECORD OF MY RESEARCH JOURNEY

| WHAT I DID AND WHY | WHAT I FOUND OUT | EVALUATION OF SOURCE AND METHOD |
|---|---|---|
|  |  |  |
|  |  |  |
|  |  |  |
|  |  |  |
|  |  |  |
|  |  |  |
|  |  |  |
|  |  |  |
|  |  |  |

**4.5**

# 4.5 KEY SKILLS

Depending on what you do and how you do it, your research should give you several opportunities for building Key Skills evidence. Completing this chart will give you some ideas.

| KEY SKILL | MAIN ELEMENTS | EVIDENCE FROM YOUR RESEARCH |
|---|---|---|
| Communication | Discussions; presentations; reading and synthesising information about complex subjects; writing documents, including extended writing. | |
| Information Technology | Planning and using different sources, using text, image and numbers; exploring, developing and exchanging information; presenting information. | |
| Application of number | Planning and interpreting information from different sources; calculating; presenting findings; explaining results; justifying choice of method. | |

You may also find that your research gives you opportunities to practise and gather evidence for the Wider Key Skills of Working With Others, Improving Your Own Learning and Problem Solving.

**4.6**

# 4.6 GLOSSARY

**Action research model** – an ongoing research model, usually referring to research carried out by someone who wants to explore, change or improve something they are already doing; e.g. a teacher might carry out action research to find other ways of teaching a particular unit.

**Archetype** – a recognisable stock character or typical example which can be created again and again, e.g. the villain and the hero.

**Demographics** – population studies.

**Effects debate** – effects of the media on its consumers.

**Ethics** – standards, morals or rules of behaviour.

**Ethnography** – participant study of the culture of a group.

**Focus group** – a small discussion group set up by a researcher to discuss particular issues/texts/topics.

**Hegemony** – to do with the dominance of certain groups over others.

**Hypothesis** – the starting point of research, a hypothesis is an idea, hunch or theory which you then test out through your research.

**Iconography** – the study of visual signs in media texts, e.g. the space-suits, planets and technology found in science fiction films.

**Ideology** – a set of beliefs, ideas and values, often shown through language, which are put forward by individuals or societies.

**Intertextuality** – a reference to one text within another, e.g. the horror film *Scream* (1996) refers to other horror films; intertextuality is sometimes seen as a feature of **postmodernism**.

**Methodology** – research methods and rules.

**Objective** – a balanced approach in which opinion, bias or partiality are absent.

**Postmodernism** – a theoretical approach, most evident from the 1980s onwards, which argues that there are no fixed rules and no clear absolutes; anything goes and anything can be invented or reinvented.

**Primary research** – research which you have carried out on your own, e.g. focus groups, textual analysis, questionnaires and interviews.

**Problematic** – a problem/issue/text which needs exploring and is expressed in the form of a proposal.

**Proposal** – a proposed plan for your research.

**Representation** – a way of showing something or someone in images and/or language; sometimes, representations have symbolic value.

**Qualitative research** – research which depends on the quality of the response, usually gained on a small scale through interviews, focus groups, etc. where thoughts, opinions and feelings are ascertained; evidence of qualitative research is generally shown through quotations.

**Quantitative research** – research which measures quantity in some way, e.g. through questionnaires, using data and statistics; evidence of quantitative research is generally shown through numbers on a large scale.

**Readings** – different ways in which audiences can respond to media texts – this approach has been credited to Stuart Hall:

> **Preferred reading** – the producer of a text wants us to read it in a particular way.

> **Negotiated reading** – we read a text in the producer's way and in our own way.

> **Oppositional reading** – we read a text in our own way.

**Reliable methodology** – can it be done again to get the same or similar results?

**Secondary research** – done by someone else, e.g. as found in a book, magazine or website.

**Stereotype** – a fixed idea about, or representation of, an individual or group within society.

**Subjective** – the opposite of objective; check if your syllabus requires you to use a subjective, or personal voice.

**Valid methodology** – do your results have some truth in them and can you make sound generalisations from your research?

---

**TOP TIP**

Show you are a media student by using specialist media terms.

!

**4.7**

# 4.7 BIBLIOGRAPHY AND WEBOGRAPHY

## Bibliography

Note how to record books in a bibliography:

> Author surname, author first name or initial, book title (in **bold and italicised**), edition (if not 1st), place of publication: publisher, year of publication.

Barry, Peter, **Beginning Theory: An Introduction to Literary and Cultural Theory**, Manchester: Manchester University Press, 2002.

Cook, Pam and Mieke, Bernink (eds), **The Cinema Book**, London: BFI, 1999.

Cousins, M., **The Story of Film**, London: Pavilion Books, 2004.

Creeber, Glen (ed.), **The Television Genre Book**, London: BFI, 2001.

Dorling Kindersley Ltd., **Cinema Year by Year 1894–2003**, London: Amber Books Ltd., 2003.

Guinness World Records, **The Guinness Book of Film**, London: Guinness World Records Ltd., 1999.

Holmes, Michele, **Television History Book**, London: BFI, 2003.

Hoskyns, Barney (ed.), **The Sound and the Fury: 40 years of Classic Rock Journalism**, London: Bloomsbury, 2003.

McGown, Alistair D. (ed.), **BFI Television Handbook 2005**, London: BFI, October 2004.

Modlenski, T., 'The search for tomorrow in today's soap operas', in **Loving with a Vengeance: Mass-Produced Fantasies for Women**, Hamden, Connecticut: Archon Books, 1982.

Neale, Stephen, **Genre**, London: BFI, 1980.

Negus, Keith, **Producing Pop**, London: Arnold (member of the Hodder Headline Group), 1992.

Nelmes, Jill (ed.), **An Introduction to Film Studies**, London: Routledge, 1996.

Robinson, Mark, **100 Greatest TV Ads**, London: Harper Collins, 2000.

Schneider, S. J. (General Editor), **1001 Movies You Must See Before You Die**, London: Cassell Illustrated, 2004.

Stewart, Colin, Lavelle, Marc and Kowaltzke, Adam, **Media and Meaning: An Introduction**, London: BFI, 2001.

Thornham, Sue (ed.), **Feminist Film Theory: A Reader**, Edinburgh: Edinburgh University Press, 1999.

Watson, James and Hill, Anne, **Dictionary of Media and Communication Studies**, London: Arnold, 2003.

Williams, K., **Understanding Media Theory**, London: Hodder, 2003.

# Webography

## Academic / Educational

www.aber.ac.uk/media/ — Media and Communications Studies at Aberystwyth University

www.britannica.com — Encyclopaedia Britannica online

www.englishandmedia.co.uk — English and Media Centre in London

www.nsfw.org.uk — National Schools Film Week, run by Film Education

www.theory.org.uk — Theory site run by David Gauntlett of University of Bournemouth

## Broadcasters

www.4rfv.co.uk — Regional Film and Video Industries Site

www.barb.co.uk — Broadcasters' Audience Research Board

www.bbc.co.uk — British Broadcasting Corporation

www.channel4.com — Channel 4 TV

www.itv.com — Commercial television network

www.rajar.co.uk — Radio Joint Audience Research Ltd.

www.sky.com — Sky TV

## Industry

www.britmovie.co.uk — Dedicated to British cinema

www.imdb.com — Internet movie database

www.mediazoo.co.uk — Industry related new media

www.mediauk.com — UK media sites

www.moviecliches.com — Fun movie clichés site

www.nintendo.com — Nintendo games industry

www.rab.co.uk — Radio Advertising Bureau

www.sony.com — Sony electronics company

## Organisations

www.artscouncil.org.uk — National development agency for arts in England

www.bbfc.co.uk — British Board of Film Classification

www.bfi.org.uk — British Film Institute

www.bufvc.ac.uk — British Universities Film and Video Council

www.culture.gov.uk — Government department for Culture, Media and Sport

www.filmcouncil.org.uk — UK Film Council

www.nmpft.org.uk — National Museum of Photography, Film and Television

www.ofcom.org.uk — UK communications industries regulator

www.qca.org.uk — Qualifications and Curriculum Authority

www.statistics.gov.uk — National Statistics Online

## The Press

www.beano.co.uk — Online children's comic

www.bfi.org.uk/sightandsound — *Sight and Sound* online film magazine

www.bitchmagazine.com — US feminist magazine

www.britishpathe.com — British Pathe Film Archive from 1896–1970

www.futurenet.co.uk — Online magazines subscription

www.guardian.co.uk — *The Guardian* newspaper

www.independent.co.uk — *The Independent* newspaper

www.media.guardian.co.uk — Media news from *The Guardian* (currently, registration is free)

www.mojo4music.com — *Mojo* music magazine

www.nme.co.uk — *New Musical Express* music magazine

www.nrs.co.uk — National Readership Survey, with data on newspaper and magazine readership

www.pcc.org.uk — Press Complaints Commission

www.qonline.co.uk — Q music magazine

www.screendigest.com — Global audiovisual media

www.screendaily.com — Global film news

www.talkingpix.co.uk — Film, tv and mass media

www.timeout.com — London listings magazine

www.wordmagazine.co.uk — *Word* music and entertainment magazine

Note: for full website references, the following model is sometimes adopted:

> AUTHOR or EDITOR, year. Title [online]. Place of publication: Publisher. Available at: <URL> [Accessed Date].

## AND JUST FOR FUN...

You might enjoy reflecting on your research journey as a snakes and ladders game, where you draw in snakes for the problems you encountered and then overcame and ladders for the successes in your research.

| 100 | 99 | 98 | 97 | 96 | 95 | 94 | 93 | 92 | 91 |
| --- | --- | --- | --- | --- | --- | --- | --- | --- | --- |
| 81 | 82 | 83 | 84 | 85 | 86 | 87 | 88 | 89 | 90 |
| 80 | 79 | 78 | 77 | 76 | 75 | 74 | 73 | 72 | 71 |
| 61 | 62 | 63 | 64 | 65 | 66 | 67 | 68 | 69 | 70 |
| 60 | 59 | 58 | 57 | 56 | 55 | 54 | 53 | 52 | 51 |
| 41 | 42 | 43 | 44 | 45 | 46 | 47 | 48 | 49 | 50 |
| 40 | 39 | 38 | 37 | 36 | 35 | 34 | 33 | 32 | 31 |
| 21 | 22 | 23 | 24 | 25 | 26 | 27 | 28 | 29 | 30 |
| 20 | 19 | 18 | 17 | 16 | 15 | 14 | 13 | 12 | 11 |
| 1 | 2 | 3 | 4 | 5 | 6 | 7 | 8 | 9 | 10 |

*And remember…keep consuming and studying the media.*

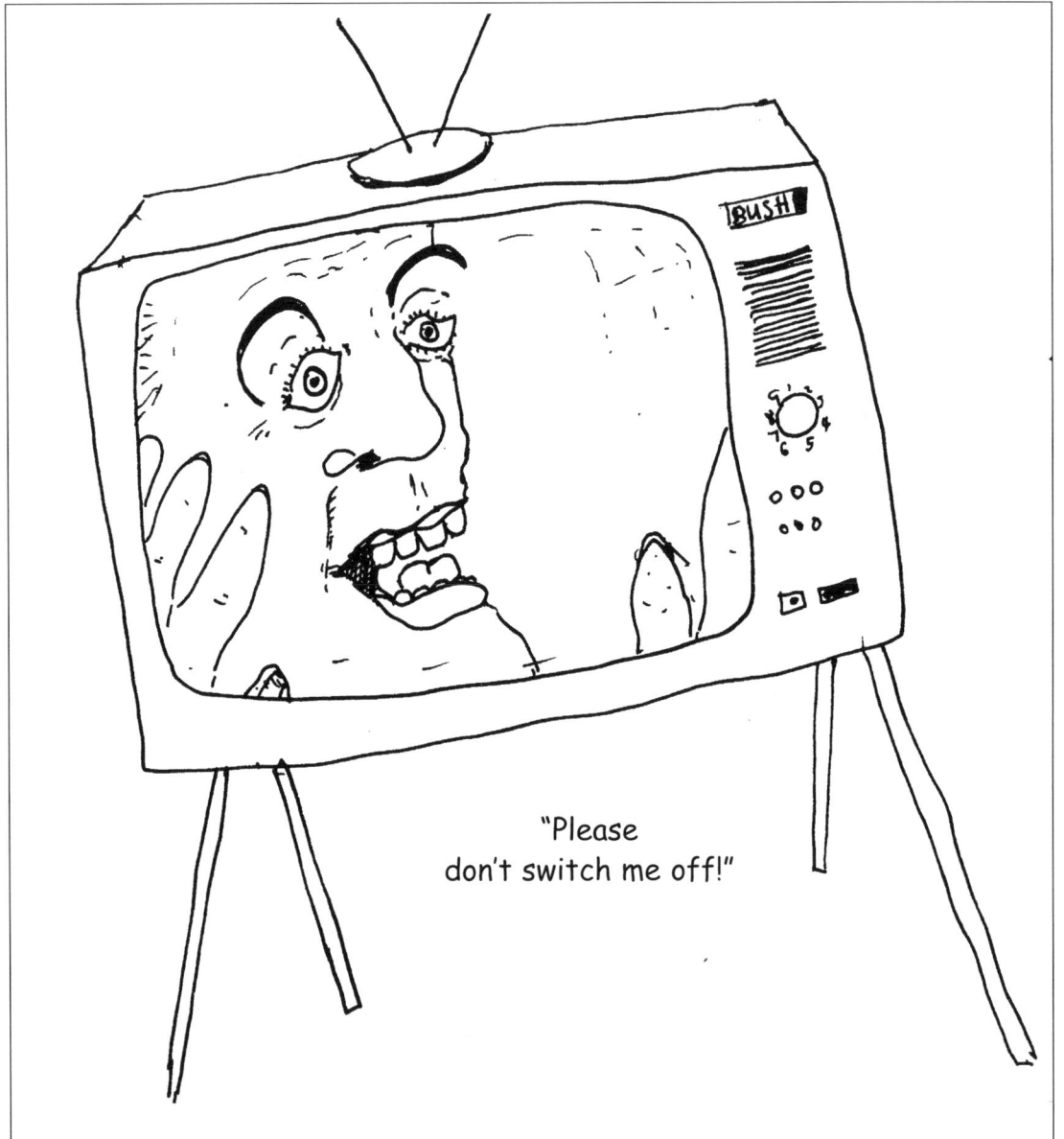